LITERATURE CONNECTIONS
SOURCEBOOK

Maniac Magee

and Related Readings

McDougal Littell
A HOUGHTON MIFFLIN COMPANY

Evanston, Illinois • Boston • Dallas

> **Links to *The Language of Literature***
>
> If you are using *Maniac Magee* in conjunction with *The Language of Literature,* please note that thematic connections can be easily made between the novel and the following units:
>
> - Grade 6, Unit 2: The Need to Belong
> - Grade 7, Unit 3: Stepping Forward
> - Grade 8, Unit 2: Critical Adjustments

Acknowledgments

Page 7: Excerpt from "Newbery Award Acceptance Speech" by Jerry Spinelli. Copyright © 1991 by the American Library Association. Reproduced with permission of the American Library Association.

Page 8: Excerpt from book review by Alison Teal in *The New York Times Book Review*, April 21, 1991. Copyright © 1991 by The New York Times Company. Reprinted by permission of The New York Times.

Page 9: Excerpt from book review by Joel Shoemaker in *School Library Journal*, June 1990. Copyright © by Cahners Publishing Company, a division of Reed Elsevier Inc. Reprinted with permission from School Library Journal.

Page 9: Excerpt from "Jerry Spinelli" by John Keller in *The Horn Book Magazine*, July 1991. Reprinted by permission of The Horn Book, Inc., 11 Beacon Street, Suite 1000, Boston, MA 02108.

Copyright © 1997 by McDougal Littell Inc. All rights reserved.

Permission is hereby granted to teachers to reprint or photocopy in classroom quantities the pages or sheets in this work that carry a McDougal Littell copyright notice. These pages are designed to be reproduced by teachers for use in their classes with accompanying McDougal Littell material, provided each copy made shows the copyright notice. Such copies may not be sold, and further distribution is expressly prohibited. Except as authorized above, prior written permission must be obtained from McDougal Littell Inc. to reproduce or transmit this work or portions thereof in any other form or by any other electronic or mechanical means, including any information storage or retrieval system, unless expressly permitted by federal copyright law. Address inquiries to Manager, Rights and Permissions, McDougal Littell Inc., P.O. Box 1667, Evanston, IL 60204.

ISBN 0-395-78354-2

34567—MAL—03 02 01

Table of Contents

Parts of the SourceBook 2
Overview Chart 3
Summaries of the Literature 4
Customizing Instruction 5

Into the Literature: *Creating Context*
    Maniac Magee 6
    The Truth About Runaways 6
    Illiteracy 6
    Spinelli's Life 7
    Spinelli on Spinelli 7
    Critic's Corner 8–9
    Literary Concepts: Characterization, Conflict, Theme 10
    Literary Concepts: Conflict 11
    Literary Concepts: Theme 12
    Motivating Activities 13

Through the Literature: *Developing Understanding*
    ***Maniac Magee* Discussion Starters** 14–17
    Related Readings Discussion Starters
        from *Freedom's Children* 18
        "Where the Rainbow Ends" 18
        "Those Who Don't" 19
        "A Lesson for Kings" 19
        "Runner" 20
        "Final Curve" 20
        "The Boy with Yellow Eyes" 21
        "Stormalong" 21
    Reproducible Pages for Students 22
        FYI: *Maniac Magee* 23–27
        FYI: from *Freedom's Children* 28
        FYI: "The Boy with Yellow Eyes" 29
        FYI: "Stormalong" 30
        FYI: Glossary 31–32
        Strategic Reading 1–4 33–36
        Literary Concept 1–3 37–39
        Vocabulary 40

Beyond the Literature: *Synthesizing Ideas*
    Culminating Writing Assignments 41
    Multimodal Activities 42–43
    Cross-Curricular Projects 44–45
    Suggestions for Assessment 46
    Test 47–48
    Test Answer Key 49–51
    Additional Resources 52–54

Parts of the SourceBook

- Table of Contents
- Overview Chart
- Summaries of the Literature
- Customizing Instruction

Into the Literature:
CREATING CONTEXT

- **Cultural/Author Background**
- **Critic's Corner** Excerpts from literary criticism about *Maniac Magee*
- **Literary Concepts**
- **Motivating Activities**

Through the Literature:
DEVELOPING UNDERSTANDING

- **Discussion Starters** Questions for the class to respond to orally after reading each section, including a Literary Concept question and a Writing Prompt
- **(FYI) FYI Pages for Students** Reproducible masters that offer students background, vocabulary help, and connections to the modern world as they read the literature
- **(FYI) Glossary** Reproducible glossary of difficult words for student use from each section of *Maniac Magee*
- **Strategic Reading worksheets** Reproducible masters to help students keep track of the plot as they read (Literal and inferential reading)
- **Literary Concept worksheets** Reproducible masters to help students understand the use of literary elements such as theme (Critical reading)
- **Vocabulary worksheet** Reproducible master to help students learn essential vocabulary used in the novel

Beyond the Literature:
SYNTHESIZING IDEAS

- **Culminating Writing Assignments** Exploratory, research, and literary analysis topics for writing, covering both the main work and the related readings
- **Multimodal Activities** Suggestions for short-term projects; some are cross-curricular.
- **Cross-Curricular Projects** Suggestions for long-term, cross-curricular, cooperative learning projects
- **Suggestions for Assessment**
- **Test, Answer Key** Essay and short-answer test on *Maniac Magee* and related readings; answer key
- **Additional Resources** Additional readings for students (coded by difficulty level) and teachers, as well as bibliographic information about commercially available technology

Overview Chart

	PAGES FOR TEACHER'S USE	PAGES FOR STUDENT'S USE
Literature Connections	**SourceBook**	**Reproducible Pages**
Maniac Magee	Customizing Instruction, p. 5 Into the Literature: Creating Context, p. 6 Critic's Corner, pp. 8–9 Literary Concepts: Characterization, Conflict, and Theme, pp. 10–12 Motivating Activities, p. 13	**FYI, p. 23** **Glossary, pp. 31–32** **Vocabulary worksheet, p. 40**
Maniac Magee Section 1, pp. 3–36	Discussion Starters, p. 14	**FYI, p. 24** **Glossary, p. 31** **Strategic Reading 1, p. 33** **Literary Concept 1, p. 37**
Maniac Magee Section 2, pp. 37–67	Discussion Starters, p. 15	**FYI, p. 25** **Glossary, p. 31** **Strategic Reading 2, p. 34** **Literary Concept 2, p. 38**
Maniac Magee Section 3, pp. 71–106	Discussion Starters, p. 16	**FYI, p. 26** **Glossary, p. 31** **Strategic Reading 3, p. 35** **Literary Concept 3, p. 39**
Maniac Magee Section 4, pp. 107–166	Discussion Starters, p. 17	**FYI, p. 27** **Glossary, p. 32** **Strategic Reading 4, p. 36**
from *Freedom's Children*, p. 173	Discussion Starters, p. 18	**FYI, p. 28**
"Where the Rainbow Ends," p. 184	Discussion Starters, p. 18	
"Those Who Don't," p. 185	Discussion Starters, p. 19	
"A Lesson for Kings," p. 186	Discussion Starters, p. 19	
"Runner," p. 188	Discussion Starters, p. 20	
"Final Curve," p. 189	Discussion Starters, p. 20	
"The Boy with Yellow Eyes," p. 190	Discussion Starters, p. 21	**FYI, p. 29**
"Stormalong," p. 200	Discussion Starters, p. 21	**FYI, p. 30**
	Culminating Writing Assignments, p. 41 Multimodal Activities, pp. 42–43 Cross-Curricular Projects, pp. 44–45 Suggestions for Assessment, p. 46 Test, Answer Key, pp. 47–51 Additional Resources, pp. 52–54	

Additional writing support for students can be found in the **Writing Coach**.

Summaries of the Literature

Maniac Magee
by Jerry Spinelli

Maniac Magee, the title character of this novel, gains instant celebrity in the town of Two Mills, Pennsylvania. Jeffrey Lionel Magee is a 12-year-old homeless wanderer who can move like no one else the town has ever seen. He earns the name "Maniac" with such feats as intercepting a football on a field of players twice his size, hitting an inside-the-park home run without a baseball, and winning a race by running backwards. As the legend of Maniac spreads, Jeffrey reluctantly takes on two challenges he can't outrun: the strong racial divisions in Two Mills and his need for a loving family. His unconventional actions weaken the town's barriers and he eventually finds the home he's always needed.

RELATED READINGS

from **Freedom's Children**
by Ellen Levine

The Civil Rights era is brought to life through the stirring accounts of individuals who were involved in the movement as young people.

Where the Rainbow Ends
by Richard Rive

Written by a South African poet during apartheid, this poem expresses the hope that brotherhood can overcome racial separation.

Those Who Don't
by Sandra Cisneros

This essay looks at both sides of a fear that often results from segregation. No matter who you are, you feel at risk in an unfamiliar neighborhood.

A Lesson for Kings
by Margaret Read MacDonald

When the two kings of this tale meet on a narrow road, the one who proves himself worthy to proceed is the one who shows his humility.

Runner
by Dona Luongo Stein

The act of running takes on a surreal quality in this poem.

Final Curve
by Langston Hughes

The speaker of this poem recognizes the difficulty of escaping the self.

The Boy with Yellow Eyes
by Gloria Gonzalez

This short story details the unlikely pairing of two boys who catch a spy in their small town during World War II.

Stormalong
by Mary Pope Osborne

In this version of the tall-tale hero's life, Stormalong is portrayed as someone who simply wants to fit in.

Customizing Instruction

Less Proficient Readers

- To help students understand the shifts in time that occur in the opening chapters of the novel, have students make a time line of Maniac Magee's life based on details the text provides. Designate the endpoint of the time line as *Meets Amanda Beale.* Then have students review the Before the Story section through Chapter 3 to find important details about Maniac that lead up to meeting Amanda.
- Throughout their reading, encourage students to keep track of the important ideas by jotting down brief summaries in their notebooks. Students may note any questions they have and make predictions about what might happen next. After students have read each of the novel's four sections, have them meet in small groups to discuss answers to questions raised in their notebooks and to check any predictions against what has actually occurred.
- Distribute photocopies of the **Glossary** (pp. 31–32) to students who may struggle with the book's vocabulary.
- Distribute photocopies of the **Strategic Reading** worksheets (pp. 33–36) to help students stay on task as they read.

Students Acquiring English

- Students can build background by discussing the novel's setting in a small American town. On the chalkboard, write two column headings: A Small Town and A Big City. Elicit responses from students by offering such points for comparison as population levels, noise levels, forms of transportation, and so on. As they read, students can compare and contrast their understanding of these concepts with the portrait of American culture presented in the novel.
- Distribute photocopies of the **Glossary** (pp. 31–32) to all students and have them check off any words they already know. On the back of each glossary page, students may keep a list of any other unfamiliar words they find as they read, noting the page numbers on which the words appear. Have students periodically meet in small groups to share their word lists, analyze unfamiliar words in the context in which they appear, and look words up in a dictionary or thesaurus.
- If appropriate, use the suggestions for Less Proficient Readers listed above.

Gifted and Talented Students

- Have students decide whether they agree with each of the Critic's Corner commentaries (pages 8–9), and then have students meet in small groups to discuss their conclusions. Students may also use a quotation from one of the commentaries as a starting point for a critical review of the novel.
- Have students note Spinelli's use of figurative language throughout the novel. Have students list their favorite examples and jot down why they think each of these is particularly effective.

Into the Literature
CREATING CONTEXT

Maniac Magee

Maniac Magee is an example of two very different literary genres: tall tale and realistic fiction. It's hard to imagine that a novel can be both at the same time, but Jerry Spinelli has found a way to successfully combine attributes of each to create a unique and spellbinding tale. Typical of tall tales, *Maniac Magee* has an omniscient narrator who addresses the reader at times, as if to make sure we are paying attention. And typical of tall tales, the hero lives an extraordinary life: he scores 49 touchdowns before dinner, jogs on a rail, and walks barefoot through a rat-infested dump. But despite all the hyperbole, Maniac is a real boy—the kind most young people long to be: resourceful, clever, funny, honest, and brave. He struggles to make sense of the real world, and so he must confront society's most complex ills: racism, parental neglect, illiteracy, and homelessness. Spinelli, however, has faith in the power of tolerance and love, and he believes in the ability of a single person to make a difference. Despite the novel's sophisticated and difficult themes, the overriding message is one of hope.

The Truth About Runaways

In *Maniac Magee,* the portrayal of life on the run is softened somewhat for a middle school audience. Jerry Spinelli alludes to "The Lost Year," the longest period of Maniac Magee's time as a runaway, but offers no details. The idea of running away appeals to the characters Russell and Piper McNab, but they don't stay away long enough to confront the reality. Several studies have shown that between 730,000 and 1.3 million children in the United States run away each year, though it's impossible to get an accurate count. Most belong to dysfunctional families and run from abusive homes, alcoholic or drug-addicted parents, or physical and sexual violence. However, it is believed that they trade one horror for another; life on the street is perilous, and children fall victim to drugs, alcoholism, AIDS, prostitution, and homicide. About 48% of runaways have attempted suicide at least once.

Illiteracy

The number of illiterate people in the United States is staggering: some sources say 40–60 million people lack basic skills in reading, writing, and arithmetic. According to author Jonathan Kozol's book *Illiterate America,* one in three people cannot read and understand this sentence. A number of factors contribute to the problem of illiteracy, but a major factor is the cycle of poverty. It is known that poor children—and one in four children lives below the poverty line—who do not have access to toys and books that teach reading readiness skills may have difficulty learning once they reach school. Also, children of illiterate parents may not get the support and assistance they need as they are learning to read.

People who are illiterate become skilled in other ways but often seek to hide their inability to read. Like Grayson in *Maniac Magee,* they may be extremely bright and competent but afraid to show what they don't know or to ask for help.

Spinelli on Spinelli

On figures of speech—

I think making similes and metaphors is fun. A lot of writing is hard work. That part of it is not necessarily easy, but it's fun. . . . [Using similes and metaphors] has to do with trying to make a vivid and effective picture of what you're trying to say. It's abstract in your head, and I never forget that what I'm trying to do is make a connection with the reader. . . . I'm building a bridge to the reader; I'm trying to touch the reader. So metaphors and similes are ways of highlighting and projecting what I see out there, so the reader can see what I'm seeing in my head; it's clarification.

QUOTED BY RAYMOND P. KETTEL IN AN INTERVIEW WITH JERRY SPINELLI, *ENGLISH JOURNAL*, SEPTEMBER 1994

On children—

Each kid is a population unto him- or herself, and a child's bedroom is as much a window to the universe as an orbiting telescope or a philosopher's study.

FROM AN AUTOBIOGRAPHICAL SKETCH IN *JUNIOR AUTHORS AND ILLUSTRATORS*

On his wish for children everywhere—

That they see their happiness not so much at the finish line, as in the running;
That they have the strength not to lift tremendous weights, but one fallen friend;
That they learn to fight their own battles with a never-ending string of temporary cease-fires;
Not that the occasion make them smile, but that their smile make the occasion;
That their bridges be built not over rivers, but over misunderstanding;
That their wealth be not in their banks, but in their hearts;
That they gain power not over others, but over themselves;
That they never fail to leave the stage before their applause is done;
That they bow not to little people with big titles, but to big people with little titles;
Not that they never know grief, but that they not know joy too soon after;
That their names be household words not throughout the land, but in their own households;
That their monuments be found not in public parks, but in the lives of those they've touched.

FROM SPINELLI'S NEWBERY AWARD ACCEPTANCE SPEECH IN *THE HORN BOOK MAGAZINE*, JULY-AUGUST 1991

Critic's Corner

CCB

CCB. *Children's Books and Their Creators*, Anita Silvey, ed. Houghton Mifflin Company, 1995.

In his many successful books for middle readers and young adults, Jerry Spinelli proves that he has accomplished what is perhaps the most important aspect of writing for children: He has stayed in touch with childhood. All of the author's books demonstrate a true genius with words. Using a spare, evocative prose resplendent with imagery and metaphor to create narrative that often borders on the poetic, Spinelli can bring the most remote setting or situation to life. Nowhere is this more evident than in the half-realistic, half-mythical tale *Maniac Magee*.

JOEL SHOEMAKER

Shoemaker, Joel. *School Library Journal*, June 1990.

Warning: this interesting book is a mythical story about racism. It should not be read as reality. . . . In the feel-good ending, Mars and Maniac resolve their differences; Maniac gets a home and there is hope for at least improved racial relations. Unreal? Yes. It's a cop-out for Spinelli to have framed this story as a legend—it frees him from having to make it real, or even possible. Nevertheless, the book will stimulate thinking about racism, and it might help educate those readers who, like so many students, have no first-hand knowledge of people of other races.

ETHEL R. TWICHELL

Twichell, Ethel R. *The Horn Book Magazine*, May-June 1990.

[Spinelli] brightens the story with exaggeration, humor, and melodrama, but avoids the feverish hilarity of his earlier books. Despite Maniac's accomplishments and the author's clear message for racial harmony, the book avoids mawkishness through the good-natured characterization of people of both races and by the vigor and clamor of their speech and actions. The book becomes, in the end, a kind of twentieth-century morality play, with Maniac a larger-than-life leader and his rag-tag companions promising, if not totally redeemed, disciples.

Critic's Corner

ALISON TEAL

Teal, Alison. *The New York Times Book Review,* **21 April 1991.**

Mr. Spinelli cautions us in his prologue not to get all bogged down in reality. . . . So right off you know there are going to be some incongruities, some slips and twists and exaggeration. It works. . . . Mr. Spinelli grapples here with a racial tension rarely addressed in fiction for children in the middle grades. To older readers the gangs in *Maniac Magee* might seem a bit toothless. The Cobras are building their bunker against the invasion of the East Enders all right, but gang members don't walk around the street with knives and handguns. There's no drug abuse, no pictures of missing children on milk cartons, no random violence in Two Mills. Maybe that's a little unreal and unsophisticated given the amount of television news children see. But the Headless Horseman that Maniac charges is the hatred that continually disrupts his world, and ours, and Mr. Spinelli . . . gives his audience a chance to smell that social contagion without the distraction of graphic violence.

JOHN KELLER

Keller, John. "Jerry Spinelli." *The Horn Book Magazine,* **July-August 1991.**

[Spinelli] gets the details right. . . . He gets it right about the fury brothers and sisters can inspire in one another as they live within a family that truly wants to function well. He gets it right about prejudice and unconditional love, and he gets it right about the magic every young person carries with him or her—a magic that shines forth if anyone takes the time to listen and observe. Jerry shows children who haven't had the edges of their personalities sanded into a smoothness that will enable them to glide more easily through life. Children, I am willing to wager, will understand at once what Maniac Magee is all about and accept him immediately as one of their own. They'll put him in that pantheon of beloved characters who become sacred points of reference when, years later, they talk about the books that meant something to them as they took that difficult, wonderful, and exciting trip through childhood.

Awards

Newbery Medal, 1991
Boston Globe/Horn Book Award, 1990

Literary Concept
CHARACTERIZATION

Characterization is the way in which writers create and develop characters' personalities. There are four basic means of character development:

1) through the character's words and actions

2) through the character's thoughts

3) through the description of the character's appearance

4) through what others think about the character

Note how Jerry Spinelli uses all four means of characterization to bring the character of George McNab to life in Chapters 35 and 39 of *Maniac Magee:*

1) Dropping the bag next to the bird remains, he [George] bellowed "Chow!" and took a beer from the fridge; he downed a good half of it in one swig, belched, doubled-clutched, and belched again.

2) He had to know someone besides himself was standing in the kitchen, and, just as obviously, he didn't care.

3) He wore no winter jacket, only a sleeveless green sweatshirt, which ballooned over his enormous stomach.

4) "We need more," growled the father [George]. John didn't answer. "We need more."

Presentation Suggestions Remind students that the ways in which writers create and develop characters' personalities are known as **characterization.** You may wish to introduce the concept by writing examples of each of the four methods of characterization on the chalkboard. Try using examples from the text of *Maniac Magee,* such as the ones shown above, or use examples from another literary work students have read.

You may wish to have students pay attention to the variety of ways they learn about the characters as they read the novel. Suggest that when students uncover new information about someone, they can note as well which technique the writer has used to convey that information. You may also wish to photocopy and distribute the **Literary Concept 1** worksheet, page 37, so that students may keep track of character development as they read.

Literary Concept
CONFLICT

In the character of Jeffrey Lionel "Maniac" Magee, Jerry Spinelli has created a legend. Despite his remarkably gentle spirit—or perhaps because of it—Maniac toughs out childhood traumas that would break the soul of a lesser boy. The novel is built around Maniac's internal and external conflicts; yet Maniac also causes conflicts between and among other characters.

In the novel, Spinelli uses Maniac as a vehicle to explore such complex social problems as homelessness, illiteracy, child abuse and neglect, and racism. Through his acts of compassion, generosity, and understanding, Maniac confronts the children and adults around him, all but demanding that they take a good hard look at their own actions, values, and prejudices.

Below are some examples of conflict in the novel.

External conflicts

- Between Maniac and society: Maniac comes into conflict with racism in the African-American community when he becomes the target of racial slurs. He faces the same conflict in the white community when he hears the bizarre and twisted impressions the McNab family has about blacks.
- Between Maniac and a force in nature: Homeless, depressed, and alone after the death of Grayson, Maniac struggles through the first bitter weeks in January to keep from starving or freezing to death.
- Between Maniac and another character: Mars Bar Thompson regards Maniac's appearance in East End, the black section of Two Mills, as a challenge to his tough-guy image.

Internal Conflicts

- Maniac is torn between staying on his own and going home with Amanda.
- Maniac is conflicted about going out on the trestle to save Russell. To do so would mean confronting his own feelings about his parents' accidental deaths.

Presentation Suggestions Remind students that **conflict** is the struggle between two opposing forces; **external conflict** can occur between a character and an outside force; **internal conflict** is a struggle within a character's mind. Discuss the kinds of conflict outlined above. Suggest that students meet in small groups, possibly after reading each of the assigned sections of the novel, to discuss the conflicts, shading in a scale like the example shown to rate the intensity of the conflicts and to compare them. You may also wish to have students complete **Literary Concept 2,** page 38, as they read.

Intensity of Conflict—Between Maniac and Mars Bar in Section 1

Low	Medium	High

Literary Concept
THEME

In his writing, Jerry Spinelli isn't afraid to tackle the problems young adolescents face as they struggle to make sense of themselves and the complex world around them. In fact, those problems are at the core of Spinelli's young adult novels, and in *Maniac Magee,* he takes on complicated social problems as well. Below are some major **themes** in the novel.

- Ignorance is the cornerstone of racial prejudice.
- There are no rules about what constitutes a family.
- It's never too late to learn.
- Friendship knows no boundaries.
- Learning occurs throughout one's life.
- Living without a home is a day-to-day struggle for survival—for both body and spirit.
- People are afraid of what they don't understand.

Presentation Suggestions You may wish to define and discuss the concept of **theme** with students before they read the novel. Remind them that a theme of a literary work is an insight about life or human nature. You might choose one or more of the themes listed above that also appears in another literary work students have read, and discuss how the message was revealed in that work. Suggest that students note how Spinelli communicates the same message as they read *Maniac Magee.* You may also wish to photocopy and distribute the **Literary Concept 3** worksheet, page 39, and have students complete the worksheet as they read.

Motivating Activities

1. **Challenging Assumptions** Ask students to remember a time when they heard about a person before actually meeting him or her. Perhaps students heard about a teacher, a new student, or a faraway relative. Suggest that students make a two-column chart in their notebooks. In the first column, have them brainstorm a list of things that they had heard were true about the person. In the second column, have them write their impressions of the person after they actually met. In small groups, students should share their charts and discuss whether what they had heard about a person affected their ability to get to know the person on his or her own terms.

2. **Linking to Today: Running Away** Begin a discussion about why young teenagers might run away from home. Together, brainstorm a list of reasons on the chalkboard. Have students think about what it would be like to live on the streets. Then explore alternatives to running away. Ask students what they know about crisis hotlines and other resources for children who need help with the sometimes difficult situations they face at home.

3. **Linking to Today: Racial Prejudice** Explain to students that racism is a dominant theme in *Maniac Magee*. Ask students if they have ever been discriminated against in any way—on the basis of age, race, religion, or social class, for example. Then ask what they believe was at the root of the discrimination they experienced. Lead them to conclude that fear was probably the cause. If your class is not ready to discuss these difficult issues aloud, have them write about their experiences in their notebooks. Students may wish to share their experiences after they've had a chance to read the novel and to discuss Maniac's experiences with prejudice.

4. **Tapping Prior Knowledge: Heroes and Legends** On the top half of a sheet of paper, have students create a word web about heroes; on the bottom half, have them create one for legends. In connecting circles, students should write words they associate with each term. After they've completed their webs, have them compare the two to see if the characteristics overlap in any way. Then lead a group discussion about what makes a hero and what makes a legend. Invite students to think about how the character Maniac Magee fits the characteristics of a hero or a legend.

5. **Resolving Conflicts** Brainstorm a class list of common conflicts students face—at school, in social situations, or at home. Then in pairs or small groups, have students choose a situation and role-play the conflict. Let students know that they must avoid shouting, name-calling, or any threats of physical violence. Instead they should create a new way to talk through a problem and solve it peaceably.

6. **Background** Reproduce and distribute the FYI page (p. 23) that gives background for *Maniac Magee*. You may also wish to reproduce and distribute all the FYI pages for the novel at this time. Encourage students to refer to these pages for additional information as they read.

Through the Literature
DEVELOPING UNDERSTANDING

BEFORE READING

> You might want to distribute
> - *p. 24, Glossary, p. 31*
> - *Strategic Reading 1, p. 33*
> - *Literary Concept 1, p. 37*

Maniac Magee

SECTION 1
Before the Story and Chapters 1–11

AFTER READING

Discussion Starters

1. What were your thoughts as you finished the first part of Maniac's story?
2. What three words would you use to describe Maniac Magee at this point?
3. What do you think about the choice of *Maniac* as a nickname for Jeffrey Lionel Magee?

> **CONSIDER**
> - ✓ how he earns the name
> - ✓ how Maniac might feel about the name— and the fame that comes with it

4. What do you think Giant John McNab and Mars Bar Thompson have in common?
5. Why do you think Maniac cares so much about what happens to Amanda's book?
6. **Literary Concept: Conflict** A conflict is a struggle between opposing forces. What are some of the conflicts you've noticed so far in *Maniac Magee?*
7. Of all the things that happen to Maniac in Section I, which seem the most unbelievable to you? Explain.
8. **Making Connections** Many people think competing—and winning—on the athletic field is very important. Are people in your school treated differently if they're good at sports? Why?

Writing Prompt

Choose four important events that take place in the life of Jeffrey Lionel Magee as it is described in Section 1 of the novel. Write a brief **summary** of each of those events.

BEFORE READING

You might want to distribute

 p. 29, Glossary, p. 31
- *Strategic Reading 2, p. 34*
- *Literary Concept 2, p. 38*

AFTER READING

SECTION 2
Chapters 12–21

Discussion Starters

1. If you could say something to Maniac at this point of the story, what would you say?
2. Maniac sleeps on the floor of Amanda's room because he "just couldn't stand being too comfortable." Why do you think this is so?
3. Why do you think Maniac breaks down and sobs, crying "I love you" in Mrs. Beale's arms after she reacts strongly to his talking trash?
4. Why do you suppose Maniac Magee couldn't see the "dislike" that was "piling up around him?"
5. In your own words, explain why the man who singles out Maniac at the block party wants Maniac to go back to the other side of town.
6. Why does Amanda's taunt about the library card have such a strong effect on Maniac?
7. How does Amanda's plan to have Maniac untie Cobble's Knot both succeed and fail?

   CONSIDER
   - ✓ what Cobble's knot might represent to the town of Two Mills
   - ✓ why she wants him to untie the knot
   - ✓ what people do while he's working
   - ✓ what happens after he unties it

8. **Literary Concept: Theme** Name any theme, or message about life or human nature, that you discovered in Section 2 of *Maniac Magee*, and explain its effect on you. Use examples from the text to support your answer.
9. **Making Connections** When people of different races don't get along, what issues besides color do you think are part of the problem?

Writing Prompt

Imagine that you are Maniac Magee and that you have just walked down the center of Hector Street right out of town. Write a **letter** to Amanda explaining your sudden departure and tell her what you think you'll do next.

SourceBook 15

BEFORE READING

You might want to distribute

 p. 26, Glossary, p. 32
- *Strategic Reading 3, p. 35*
- *Literary Concept 3, p. 39*

SECTION 3

Chapters 22–32

AFTER READING

Discussion Starters

1. How did you react to the death of Grayson?
2. What kind of a man is Grayson?

CONSIDER

✓ how he treats Maniac

✓ the questions he asks about the Beales

✓ his description of his youth

✓ what he knows—and doesn't know—how to do

3. Were you surprised by Maniac's decision not to move in with Grayson at the YMCA? Why or why not?
4. **Literary Concept: Characterization** How does the author make the characters of Grayson and Maniac come alive in Section 3? Look for physical descriptions of the characters, examples of the characters' actions or of the things they say or think, and examples of the narrator's direct comments about the characters.
5. How would you describe Maniac and Grayson's life together?
6. How do you think Maniac will cope with Grayson's death?
7. **Making Connections** What has meeting Grayson in this part of *Maniac Magee* taught you about illiteracy? Explain.

Writing Prompt

In the months they spend together, both Maniac and Grayson learn many things. Create a **comparison chart** of what they learn. Fold a sheet of paper in half and fill in information under the chart headings shown below

What Grayson learns from Maniac	What Maniac learns from Grayson

16 Literature Connections

BEFORE READING

You might want to distribute

 p. 27, Glossary, p. 32
- *Strategic Reading 4, p. 36*

SECTION 4

Chapters 33–46

AFTER READING

Discussion Starters

1. What did you think of the novel's ending?
2. Why do you suppose Maniac feels as he does at the end of Chapter 33?
3. Why do you think Maniac cares so much about influencing Russell and Piper in positive ways?
4. Why does Maniac wonder whether he's the orphan when he's in the McNabs' household?
5. **Literary Concept: Internal Conflict** How do you account for Maniac's mixed reactions after he beats Mars Bar in the race?
6. **Making Connections** Feeling important seems to be key to Russell and Piper's success and happiness. What motivates you to succeed?

Writing Prompt

Imagine that you are Maniac Magee and you're getting ready to curl up to go to sleep on Amanda's bedroom floor on your first night back in their home. Write the **diary entry** you might write before you fall asleep.

BEFORE READING

You might want to distribute
 p. 28

RELATED READINGS

from Freedom's Children

AFTER READING

Discussion Starters

1. Which of the children's stories made the strongest impression on you? Why?
2. Several of the children in the selection found ways to protest segregation and racism publicly. Find specific examples in the selection, and tell what you thought about their actions.
3. What was your reaction as you read about Reverend Fred Shuttlesworth's sermon after his home was bombed, page 177?
4. On page 178, Thelma Eubanks says that she was not afraid after she got involved in the civil rights movement. How might getting involved make a person feel less afraid of the frightening and dangerous racist activities going on in a community?
5. The excerpt from *Freedom's Children* describes the civil rights movement and what it was like to be an African-American child during the 1950s and 1960s. How does the excerpt affect your understanding of the characters in *Maniac Magee*, a novel that takes place 20 years later?

Writing Prompt

Myrna Carter says, "We felt that being free was being able to go where you wanted to go, do what you wanted to do, without fear." Write your own **definition** of freedom, using Myrna's statement as a starting point if you wish. Be sure to tell whether you are free according to your definition.

Where the Rainbow Ends

AFTER READING

Discussion Starters

1. What do you imagine the music at the end of the rainbow sounds like?
2. Do you think the speaker is positive or negative about the future? Explain your answer.
3. What do you think it will take for people of all colors to learn to "sing the same tune"?
4. Some people believe that the end of the rainbow is a mystical place where dreams come true. Do you think that Maniac Magee would share the speaker's dream about life at the end of the rainbow? Why or why not?

Writing Prompt

Write a **poem** about what you think lies at the rainbow's end.

Those Who Don't

AFTER READING

Discussion Starters

1. What were you left thinking at the end of the selection?
2. What kind of person is the narrator, the one expressing the ideas? Use evidence from the selection to support your ideas.
3. What do you suppose the narrator would want the people who get lost and come into her neighborhood by mistake to know about her and her neighbors?
4. Were you surprised to learn that the narrator feels afraid to go into a "neighborhood of another color"? Why or why not?
5. What effect does the last line, "That is how it goes and goes," have on you?
6. How does life in the narrator's community compare with Maniac Magee's life in the East End and West End of Two Mills?

Writing Prompt

Do you and the narrator have anything in common? Is your experience similar or completely different? Have you ever been lost in an unfamiliar neighborhood? What happened? Write a **personal response** to this selection in which you answer one or more of these questions.

A Lesson for Kings

AFTER READING

Discussion Starters

1. What is your reaction to this tale?
2. What do you think it says about both kings that they held to the middle ground instead of moving over to let each other pass?
3. Do you agree with the charioteer of Benares that Kosala's virtues sound more like faults? Why or why not?
4. In your own words, describe the virtues of the King of Benares.
5. Read the explanation of the Gordian Knot on FYI page 25. Which king would most likely be able to untie this knot? Explain your responses.
6. Do you think that Maniac Magee is more like the King of Kosala or like the King of Benares? Why?

Writing Prompt

Pretend you are an on-the-scene reporter who witnesses the kings' encounter. Write a **television news report** of what takes place.

Runner

AFTER READING

Discussion Starters

1. What words or phrases in the poem stand out most in your mind?
2. What do you think of the speaker of this poem?
3. What do images of nature in the first stanza tell you about "the rules of this life"?
4. In the second stanza, what happens to remind the runner that he or she has forgotten the season?
5. Do you think that Maniac Magee ever feels the same way the speaker in this poem feels? When?

Writing Prompt

Imagine that you could meet Dona Luongo Stein, the author of "Runner." What would you talk about? Write the **dialogue** of a conversation that the two of you might have, using the poem as a jumping-off point for your conversation.

Final Curve

AFTER READING

Discussion Starters

1. What do you think it means to "turn a corner"?
2. Should rounding the final curve be seen as positive or negative? Explain your opinion.
3. How do the ideas presented in this poem connect to what happens in *Maniac Magee*?

Writing Prompt

Write a short saying or **proverb** that is based on the poem.

BEFORE READING

You might want to distribute
(FYI) *p. 29*

AFTER READING

Discussion Starters

The Boy with Yellow Eyes

1. What did you find most surprising about this story? Why?
2. Why do you think everyone agreed that "Norman was the least likely of heroes"?
3. It took two boys to catch the spy in the story. Could either Norman or Willie have caught the spy on his own? Why or why not?
4. What do you think is the main theme, or message, of this story?
5. How would you describe the friendship Norman and Willie share as adults?
6. What do you think Maniac Magee has in common with Willie and Norman?

Writing Prompt

Imagine that you are a reporter for the *Preston Heights Tribune,* and write a **newspaper account** about the Vice President's trip to town. Remember that most news stories answer the questions *who, what, when, where, why,* and *how.* Be sure to include information about Norman and Willie's adventure as you explain what happened on this special day.

BEFORE READING

You might want to distribute
 p. 30

AFTER READING

Discussion Starters

Stormalong

1. What detail from the story stands out most in your mind?
2. What seemed real or true about Stormy?
3. What seemed false or exaggerated about him?
4. Why do you suppose Stormy loved the ocean so much?
5. The book *Maniac Magee* and the tall tale "Stormalong" are both about personal journeys. What do you think Maniac and Stormy both hope to find?

Writing Prompt

Imagine that you are Stormy, working as a farmer in Kansas. Write a **postcard message** to your friends, the crew of *The Lady of the Sea.* Tell them what you are doing and how you are enjoying your new line of work. Also tell them what your goals are and ask for any help you might need in achieving them.

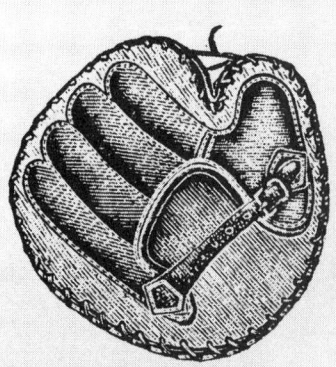

These pages for the students give background, explain references, help with vocabulary words, and help students make connections to the world of *Maniac Magee*. You can reproduce these pages and allow students to read them before or while they are reading the works in *Literature Connections*.

Table of Contents

Background 23

Section 1: Before the Story–Chapter 11 24

Section 2: Chapters 11–21 25

Section 3: Chapters 22–32 26

Section 4: Chapters 33–46 27

from *Freedom's Children* 28

"The Boy with Yellow Eyes" 29

"Stormalong" 30

Glossary 31–32

Maniac Magee

BACKGROUND

A Legend in the Making

Today, when musicians or professional athletes become widely known for their talents, skills, or achievements, we often say that they've become legends in their own time. How many legends of today can you name? A legend is actually a story that's handed down from the past—it tells about something that really happened or about a person who really lived. Sometimes the legend exaggerates the facts about the person, and the truth even stretches to make a more exciting story. With a partner, share everything you know about the American legendary heroes listed here. Can you separate the facts from the fiction?

- Johnny Appleseed (1774–1845), pioneer planter
- Davy Crockett (1786–1836), hunter, scout, soldier, and congressman
- John Henry (dates unknown), railroad laborer
- Amelia Earhart (1898–1937?), pioneer aviator

Modern Transportation—the Old-Fashioned Way

If you live in Boston, Philadelphia, or San Francisco, the words *trolley* and *trestle* are probably as familiar to you as *car, bus,* or *train*. A trolley is a streetcar, a vehicle that runs on rails that are laid in city streets. Beginning in the late 1800s and well into the 1900s, trolleys provided transportation in many major U.S. cities. Other forms of mass transit have replaced most trolleys today. Modern trolleys are usually powered by electrical cables suspended overhead or by an electrified third rail.

A trestle is similar to a bridge. It's a structure that supports a railroad track or a roadway that must cross over a valley, river, or road. A trestle is made from a horizontal beam or bar supported by two pairs of legs, or posts.

Who Is Maniac Magee?

The inspiration for this book's main character comes from an old friend of Jerry Spinelli's who was raised in an orphanage. As a boy, this friend ran everywhere he went—and when he wasn't running to or from a place, he just ran. Two or three times a week, he ran to Tony and Pete's Hoagie Hut, because sandwiches were free there for children from the orphanage. One day the author's friend learned firsthand the bitter truth about racial prejudice and segregation when he went to a swimming pool with other boys from the orphanage. Because he was African American, he was not allowed in the pool. As you read the novel, think about similarities you see between Spinelli's friend and the main character.

Chapters 1–11

SECTION 1

Maniac's Travels

As you continue reading the novel, refer to this map to help you visualize Maniac's journey. Two Mills, Pennsylvania, the main setting Jerry Spinelli describes, is imaginary, but most of the other places he mentions are real. Two Mills might be based on Norristown, Jerry Spinelli's birthplace.

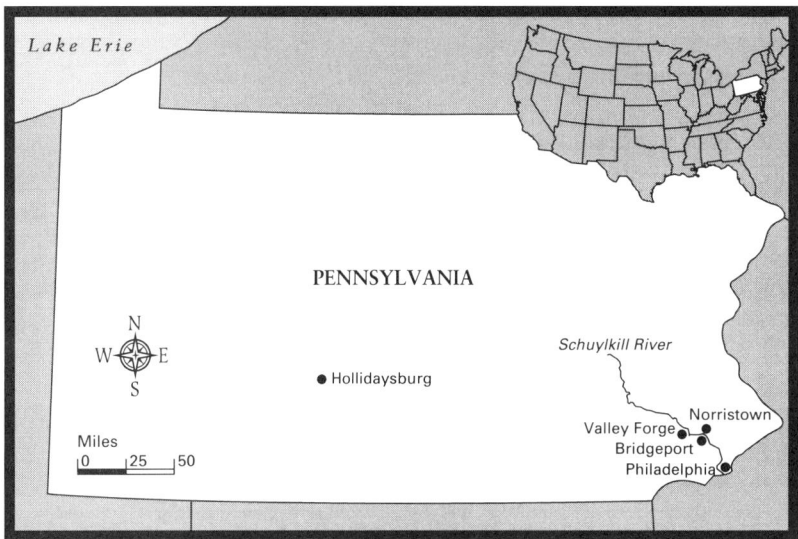

The Real Beale

Several years before Jerry Spinelli wrote *Maniac Magee*, he gave a talk at a library in New York. Afterward, he was introduced to a sixth-grade student who carried all her books to school with her in a suitcase every day. That girl became the model for the character Amanda Beale.

A Helping Hand

What can you do to help the homeless in your community?

- Raise money for a shelter or a program for homeless children. Donate food, blankets, and clothing.
- Volunteer your time in a soup kitchen or shelter.
- Be a friend. Arrange a storytime event for a group of younger children at a homeless shelter. Read aloud one of the books mentioned in *Maniac Magee* (*Lyle, Lyle, Crocodile* or *The Little Engine That Could*) or one of your own favorites.

Two Children's Crusades

Amanda lends Maniac a book on the subject of the Children's Crusade. Here's information about what might have been in Amanda's book:

- The first Children's Crusade took place in the summer of A.D. 1212. Nearly 100,000 children from France and Germany set out on foot for Jerusalem, a holy city in the land that is now Israel. For more than 100 years, European Christians had been fighting the Moslems for control of Jerusalem in a series of wars called the Crusades. The children believed they could defend their faith. Their leader was a brave and devout 12-year-old boy. The children suffered terribly on the journey, and more than 30,000 of them died. None of them reached Jerusalem.

- Another event called the Children's Crusade was organized in the name of justice. During the spring of 1963 in the U.S., a number of civil-rights demonstrations ended violently when police unleashed their dogs on the marchers and firefighters knocked marchers down with high-powered water hoses. Young people fighting for what they believed in were wounded, and thousands of teenagers were arrested and jailed. Across the nation, images of these actions were printed in newspapers and broadcast on TV, motivating others to support the cause of equal rights.

Chapters 12–21

SECTION 2

Chapter 14
Character Links to Memories

According to Jerry Spinelli, years, even decades, can pass between an experience he has and his retelling of that experience in one of his novels. When Spinelli was a little boy, he met his mother's dentist, Dr. Winters. The dentist was kind to the boy, and he lifted him into the chair and pretended to examine him. As an adult, Spinelli still remembers the wonderful way the doctor's "sure and sturdy fingers" felt inside his mouth. Years later, the memory of Dr. Winters inspired the relationship between Maniac and Mrs. Beale, whose warm brown thumb "appeared from under the creamy white icing that she allowed him to lick away when she was frosting his favorite cake."

Chapter 15
Talkin' Trash

"Trash talkin'" has become a common language in basketball, spoken on the playground as well on major-league courts. Players talk trash by calling their opponents names, making empty threats, and boasting about their ability to outscore them. The point of all this talk is to intimidate or scare opposing players and to put their mental toughness to the test. Just as Maniac discovers there's a price to be paid for talkin' trash, professional players are learning that trash talk isn't always cheap. There are new rules against using verbal taunts during a game, and some kinds of trash talk can result in a technical foul, a fine, or even suspension.

Chapter 19
Solving a Knotty Problem

Cobble's Knot, a legend in Two Mills, bears a striking resemblance to a well-known knot of ancient times: the Gordian Knot. In about the 8th century B.C., Gordius, the king of Phrygia (frĭj′ ē-ə)—a region that's now part of Turkey—tied an incredibly complicated knot to his chariot. No one could see the beginning or the end of the knot. According to legend, whoever untied the knot would conquer and rule all of Asia. When the king of Macedonia, Alexander the Great, came through the region around 333 B.C., he tried unsuccessfully to untie the knot. Finally, he solved the problem by taking out his sword and cutting the knot into pieces! Alexander did go on to rule all of Asia. Today, a "Gordian knot" refers to a difficult problem, and the expression "cutting the Gordian knot" means solving the problem easily or with sheer force.

Chapters 22–23

SECTION 3

The Old Ball Game
- There are two major baseball leagues: the American league and the National League.
- The minor league is the training ground for major league players.
- There are 17 minor leagues with about 175 teams in the United States, Canada, and Mexico.
- The minor leagues are divided into classifications: Class A, Class AA, and Class AAA. There are also rookie leagues, where players often start out. The triple A league is the last stop before the majors.
- In the Little League, players range in age from six to eighteen or so. The rules of play differ from rules for major leaguers, playing fields are smaller, and games may be fewer than nine innings.

It's Fun to Stay at the YMCA

The Young Men's Christian Association, or YMCA, was founded in England in 1844. For many years, membership has been open to people of all ages, religions, races, and incomes. More than half of the YMCA's 25 million members live in the U.S. Some YMCAs provide people with inexpensive places to live. Other YMCAs have gymnasiums and fitness centers and run special programs for teenagers and their families. The "Y" hopes that by participating in its programs, people will

- live a more active lifestyle.
- relax with their families.
- develop leadership skills.
- learn more about others.
- help improve neighborhoods.

Chapter 25
Major Major-Leaguer

Willie Mays, the player whom Grayson says he struck out in Mays's last at-bat in the minors, went on to become one of the most exciting players of all time. Nicknamed the "Say Hey Kid" for the way he liked to greet others, Mays excelled in hitting, fielding, and base running. His 660 career home runs place him at the level of such legends as Babe Ruth and Hank Aaron. Mays was a major-league player from the early 1950s to the early 1970s. He was inducted into baseball's Hall of Fame in 1979.

Chapter 26
The Stopball: The Real Story

The inspiration for Grayson's special pitch was the baseball coach who trained Jerry Spinelli from the time the author was 13 years old. During batting practice, Skag Cottman would throw the "stopball," permitting Jerry and his teammates a single chance to hit it each day. "It comes up to the plate all big and fat," Skag told the boys. "Then it stops and waits for you to swing, and then it goes on to the catcher's mitt." According to Spinelli, the stopball struck the boys out every time.

Chapters 33–46

SECTION 4

Chapter 33
The "Winter of Despair"

During the Revolutionary War (1775–1782), young men joined the Continental Army, formed by the American Congress to fight the British for independence. In September, 1777, the British took control of the city of Philadelphia. General George Washington then led his defeated troops to Valley Forge, an area along the Schuylkill River about 25 miles northwest of the city. The men camped there during the long, bitter winter of 1777 and 1778. During this period, which became known as the "Winter of Despair," an estimated 2,500 soldiers, or one quarter of Washington's troops, died of starvation, frostbite, or disease.

Chapter 33
Salvation Army

The Salvation Army, an international Christian religious and charitable organization, raises money to help the needy. It was founded in 1865, and it runs more than 14,000 community centers in over 85 countries. The Salvation Army also runs "soup kitchens," places where food is prepared and served to the homeless or to the very poor.

Making Peace

Maniac Magee often finds himself face to face with someone who opposes him. The next time you find yourself in a conflict, try these techniques:

- Set aside time to talk about the problem.
- Ask a neutral person to help mediate, or solve, the problem.
- Agree to keep talking until a solution to the problem is found.
- Agree to speak one at a time—no interrupting!
- Take turns telling what happened. Repeat what the other person says in your own words to make sure you understand that person's point of view. Have the neutral person say back what he or she is hearing you say.
- Brainstorm a list of possible solutions and choose a solution that both sides can agree to.
- Discuss what you could do differently next time.

It's BISON, You Buffalo!

Bison, or American bison, is the correct name for the great herds that once roamed wild across North America. Here are more facts about American bison:

- Bison have larger heads and necks than buffalo.
- A bison has 14 pairs of ribs, while a buffalo has 13 pairs.
- A bison has humped shoulders.
- In 1850 about 20 million bison lived in North America. By 1889 white hunters had slaughtered so many bison that only 541 were living.
- About 15,000 bison now live in game preserves in the U.S.

SourceBook 27

from Freedom's Children
BY ELLEN LEVINE

The Constitution

In his interview about the civil-rights era, Larry Russell shares his thoughts about the Constitution. Signed in 1787, and in effect since 1789, the Constitution of the United States states the laws of the nation, defines the role of government, and summarizes the rights and freedoms of the American people. These amendments or changes to the Constitution were the first to directly affect the lives of African Americans:

- **The 13th amendment (1865)**
  —Abolished slavery.

- **The 14th amendment (1868)**
  —Made former slaves citizens of the United States and of the states in which they lived.

- **The 15th amendment (1870)**
  —States that a person cannot be denied the right to vote on account of race, color, or previous condition of servitude. Even so, many states passed laws to prevent voting; in the early 1900s, those laws were declared unconstitutional.

The Preamble

Each day as a child, Larry Russell had to recite the preamble or the introduction to the Constitution. The preamble appears in these words:

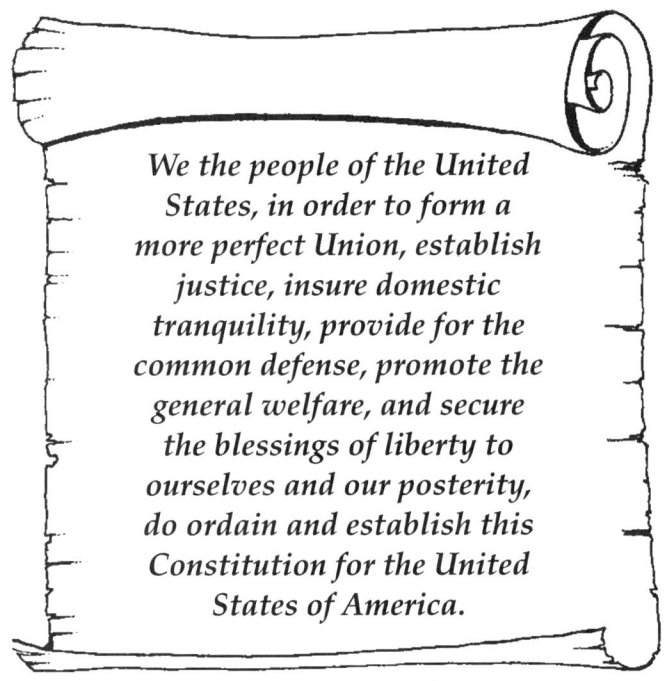

We the people of the United States, in order to form a more perfect Union, establish justice, insure domestic tranquility, provide for the common defense, promote the general welfare, and secure the blessings of liberty to ourselves and our posterity, do ordain and establish this Constitution for the United States of America.

Forms of Protest

During the 1950s and 1960s, people all over the U.S. began to speak out against segregation, the policy and practice of forcing racial groups to live in separate places, attend separate schools, and so on. Protests were common. Here are some forms that their protests took.

- **boycott:** an act of protest in which people unite with others in refusing to use, buy, or deal with a person or product.

- **demonstration:** a march, rally, or other public display of group opinion.

- **sit-in:** an organized demonstration in which people sit down in an appropriate place and refuse to move. African Americans participated in sit-ins at lunch counters and other public places that separated races by sitting in seats marked "whites only."

The Boy with Yellow Eyes

BY GLORIA GONZALES

Norman's Choices

From Norman's point of view in "The Boy with Yellow Eyes," the experience of reading a book is every bit as dynamic as playing baseball. Here's information about the books and characters that Norman mentions:

- Tom Sawyer and Huck Finn appear in the classic American novels *The Adventures of Tom Sawyer* and *The Adventures of Huckleberry Finn* by Mark Twain (whose real name was Samuel Langhorne Clemens).

- *Dracula,* the classic story of a human vampire who stays alive by sucking blood from his victims, was written by Irish author Bram Stoker. It was published in 1897, 12 years after *The Adventures of Huckleberry Finn.*

Know the Code

Samuel Finley Breese Morse arrived in London, England, from Massachusetts in 1811. In a letter to his mother, he wrote:

> I wish that in one instant I could tell you of my safe arrival, but we are 3,000 miles apart and must wait four long weeks to hear from each other.

Twenty-one years later, Morse made his wish come true by inventing a system for sending messages electronically. Working long and hard, he perfected a device and created a telegraphic code that could be used to send messages. In 1854 Morse received a patent for the telegraph, and the code he created still bears his name. In Morse code, sequences of dots and dashes, or short and long signals, represent numbers and letters of the alphabet. Today, radio operators, ships at sea, and the military still use the code.

Eye on the FBI

The Federal Bureau of Investigation, or FBI, is a branch of the United States Department of Justice. The bureau's main office is in Washington, D.C., but there are branch offices in major cities across the country. FBI investigators, or special agents, try to solve federal crimes, such as bank robbery, kidnapping, hijacking, and bombing. Agents help local police departments find criminals. They also gather information about people who are believed to be dangerous to the country's security, such as those who organize riots, threaten to overthrow the government, or reveal top-secret information to foreign governments.

Stormalong

BY MARY POPE OSBORNE

Armed and Dangerous?

About 50 different kinds of octopuses swim in oceans around the world. An octopus has a rounded soft body and eight tentacles, or arms. Each tentacle bears two rows of suckers. Octopuses are carnivorous, or flesh-eating, and can be quite dangerous. Could a man—even a strong man like Stormalong—really wrestle a two-ton octopus? Could he even *find* a two-ton octopus? What a tall tale! The largest octopus measures nine or ten feet long and weighs only about 70 pounds.

Stormy's Historic Roots

Alfred Bulltop Stormalong was invented by sailors who worked out of the ports of New England in the early to mid-1800s. In those days, the sea was extremely important to Americans, as tens of thousands of people earned their livelihood from it. Life on the ocean was dangerous, however, and survival was a continuous challenge. The legendary Stormalong, through his sheer size and strength, was able to conquer and control nature—something real sailors could never do.

Look over Dover

If you ever cross the English Channel on a ferry, you're bound to pass through Dover, the most important port on the English side of the Channel and the closest one to France. The port at Calais, France, is only 22 miles (or 35 kilometers) away. Once on board the ferry, you'll be able to see the famous cliffs, made white from chalk. When microscopic, one-celled animals called foraminifera die and sink to the bottom of the sea, their shells mix with lime mud to form chalk deposits. The chalk in Dover's cliffs was formed during the Cretaceous period some 135 million years ago. Or you may prefer to believe it's the soap from the sides of Stormalong's clipper ship!

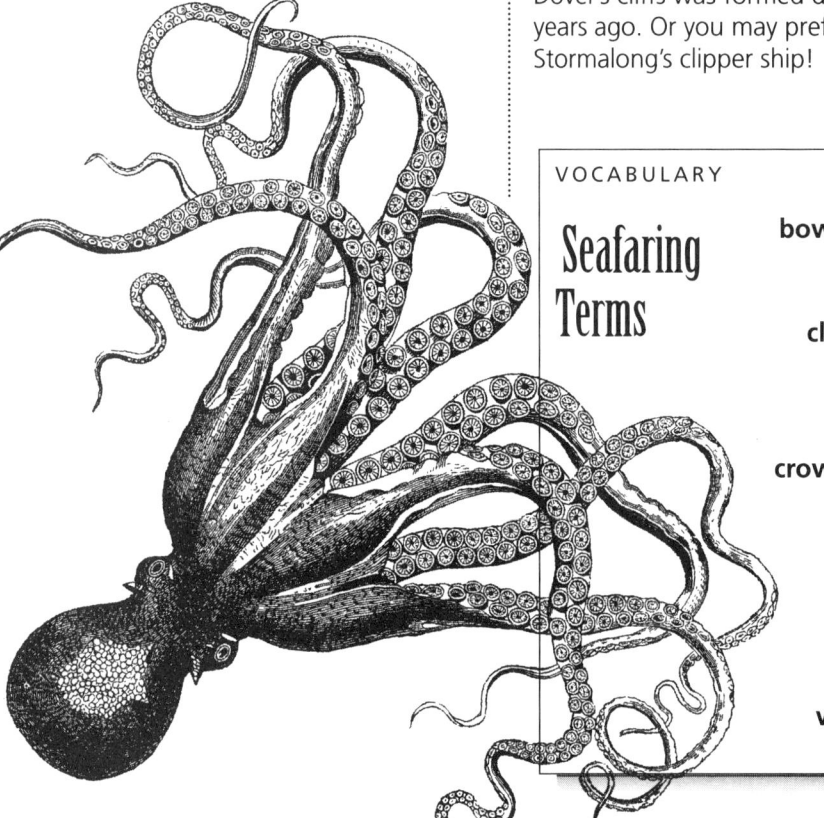

VOCABULARY

Seafaring Terms

bowsprit	a wooden pole extending forward from the front end of a ship, to which a mast may be fastened
clipper	a sharp-bowed sailing vessel of the mid-19th century, having tall masts and sharp lines and built for great speed
crow's-nest	a small lookout platform with a protective railing, located near the top of a ship's mast
mast	a tall pole that rises from the deck of a ship to support the sails
port	a city or town on a waterway where ships may dock
wharf	a landing place or pier where ships may tie up and load or unload

Glossary

MANIAC MAGEE

Section 1: Chapters 1–11

befuddled (bĭ-fŭd' ld): *adj.* confused *p. 32*

blunder (blŭn' dər): *v.* move blindly, by mistake *p. 16*

commotion* (kə-mō' shən): *n.* disturbance *p. 16*

gangplank (găng' plăngk'): *n.* board or ramp forming a bridge between a ship and a pier; pirates used to make their victims walk the gangplank—into the sea *p. 22*

infamous* (ĭn'fə-məs): *adj.* having a bad reputation; unfavorably well-known *p. 16*

legacy* (lĕg' ə-sē): *n.* something handed down *p. 4*

lumber* (lŭm' bər): *v.* walk with heavy clumsiness *p. 24*

midst (mĭdst): *n.* middle *p. 8*

pandemonium (păn' də-mō' nē-əm): *n.* wild uproar or noise *p. 23*

scraggly* (skrăg' lē): *adj.* ragged; untidy *p. 9*

stupefied* (stoō' pə-fī'd): *adj.* amazed; stunned *p. 18*

theory* (thē' ə-rē): *n.* guess; idea *p. 9*

wretch (rĕch): *n.* a miserable, unfortunate, or unhappy person *p. 16*

Section 2: Chapters 12–21

contortion (kən-tôr' shən): *n.* a distortion, twist, or unusual bend *p. 62*

converge* (kən-vûrj'): *v.* come together from different directions; meet *p. 45*

eon (ē'ŏn'): *n.* a long period of time *p. 61*

hemisphere* (hĕm' i-sfîr'): *n.* half of the earth *p. 40*

pulpit (poŏl' pĭt): *n.* a lectern or stand used during a religious service *p. 44*

solitude* (sŏl' ĭ-toōd'): *n.* the state of being alone *p. 44*

Section 3: Chapters 22–32

abruptly* (ə-brŭpt' lē): *adv.* unexpectedly and suddenly *p. 79*

bide (bīd): *v.* await *p. 101*

consciousness* (kŏn' shəs-nĭs): *n.* awareness of one's self *p. 94*

disperse* (dĭ-spûrs'): *v.* spread out in different directions *p. 99*

geezer (gē'zər): *n.* an eccentric or unconventional old man *p. 88*

gingerly* (jĭn'jər-lē): *adv.* cautiously *p. 92*

grizzled (griz'əld): *adj.* partly gray *p. 87*

immortality* (ĭm'ô-răl'ĭ-tē): *n.* enduring or lasting fame *p. 85*

meander (mē-ăn'dər): *v.* wander along, taking a winding course *p. 101*

preposterous (prĭ-pŏs'tər-əs): *adj.* foolish or absurd *p. 94*

pungent* (pŭn'jənt): *adj.* sharp-smelling *p. 100*

repertoire (rĕp'ər-twär): *n.* the range of skills or techniques of a person *p. 87*

rickety* (rĭk'ĭ-tē): *adj.* shaky, unsteady *p. 87*

stoic* (stō'ĭk): *adj.* unaffected by pain or pleasure *p. 104*

PRONUNCIATION KEY

ă	at, gas	îr	dear, here	th	thing, with
ā	ape, day	ng	sing, anger	th	then, other
ä	father, barn	ŏ	odd, not	ŭ	up, nut
âr	fair, dare	ō	open, road, grow	ûr	fur, earn, bird, worm
ĕ	egg, ten	ô	awful, bought, horse	zh	treasure, garage
ē	evil, see, meal	oi	coin, boy	ə	awake, even, pencil, pilot, focus
hw	white, everywhere	oŏ	look, full	ər	perform, letter
ĭ	inch, fit	oō	root, glue, through		
ī	idle, my, tried	ou	out, cow		

SOUNDS IN FOREIGN WORDS

kh	*German* ich, auch; *Scottish* loch	œ	*French* feu, cœur; *German* schön	ü	*French* utile, rue; *German* grün
n	*French* entre, bon, fin				

* The words followed by asterisks are useful words that you might add to your vocabulary.

SourceBook **31**

Glossary (continued)

MANIAC MAGEE

Section 4: Chapters 33–46

amble (ăm′bəl): *v.* walk slowly, leisurely *p. 119*

beseech* (bĭ-sēch′): *v.* beg *p. 111*

carrion (kăr′ē-ən): *n.* dead and decaying flesh *p. 119*

desolation (dĕs′ə-lā′shən): *n.* the state of being abandoned *p. 110*

diverge* (dĭ-vûrj′): *v.* go in different directions; separate *p. 155*

extort (ĭk-stôrt): *v.* to get by misusing power with threats, force, or intimidation *p. 139*

exuberance (îg-zōō′bər-əns): *n.* the state of being extremely enthusiastic and happy *p. 132*

gaunt (gônt): *adj.* thin and bony *p. 111*

ludicrous* (lōō′dĭ-krəs): *adj.* ridiculous enough to be laughable *p. 135*

maraud (ma-rôd′): *v.* rove and wander in search of goods to steal *p. 136*

nonchalantly* (nŏn′shə-länt′lē): *adv.* in an unconcerned or indifferent manner *p. 119*

pillbox (pĭl′bŏks′): *n.* a low-roofed concrete building at a strategic military site with openings for machine guns *p. 135*

portal (pôr′tl): *n.* doorway *p. 124*

prone* (prōn): *adj.* lying face downward *p. 120*

succession (sək-sĕsh′ən): *n.* in sequence, one after the other *p. 112*

surge* (sŭrj): *v.* swell and move forward like a wave *p. 132*

warily* (wer′ə-lē): *adv.* cautiously *p. 114*

* The words followed by asterisks are useful words that you might add to your vocabulary.

32 Literature Connections

Name _____

SECTION 1, BEFORE THE STORY—CHAPTER 11

Understanding Characters' Actions

To understand the characters in *Maniac Magee,* think about what causes them to do what they do. Read the actions listed in the left column. Then, in the right column, write the reasons for the actions, as you see them. The first one is done for you as an example.

Character and Action	Possible Reasons
Amanda lends a book to Jeffrey Magee.	Jeffrey Magee looks lonely and in need of a worthwhile way to spend his time.
Jeffrey performs several amazing feats, never letting go of Amanda's book.	
The Cobras stop chasing Maniac when he crosses from the west to the east of Hector Street.	
Mars Bar snatches away the book that Maniac is holding.	
Maniac at first sleeps on the floor of his room at the Beales' home.	
Maniac leaves the Beale home after unravels Cobble's Knot.	

SourceBook 33

Name _____

Strategic Reading ②
SECTION 2, CHAPTERS 12–21

Identifying Cause and Effect

Two events are related as cause and effect if one brings about, or causes, the other. The event that happens first is the cause; the one that follows is the effect. Fill in the blanks for each chapter listed below. You may need to write the cause of a stated effect, or the effect of a stated cause.

Chapter	Cause	Effect
12		Mr. Beale makes a U-turn and brings Maniac back home with him.
15	Maniac fits in with the other kids by learning to talk trash.	
17		Someone writes a message on the Beales' house.
18		Maniac goes out for a long run in the morning and doesn't return until late that night.
19	Amanda wants Maniac to become a hero to people living on both sides of town.	
21	Someone turns Amanda's encyclopedia into confetti.	

34 Literature Connections

Name _____

Strategic Reading ③
SECTION 3, CHAPTERS 22–32

Comparing and Contrasting Characters

One way to learn about characters in your reading is to compare and contrast them with other characters. How are they alike? How are they different? What do characters have in common and what sets them apart from one another? Use the Venn diagram below to compare and contrast Grayson and Maniac Magee. Remember to record the characters' similarities in the intersecting part of the two circles.

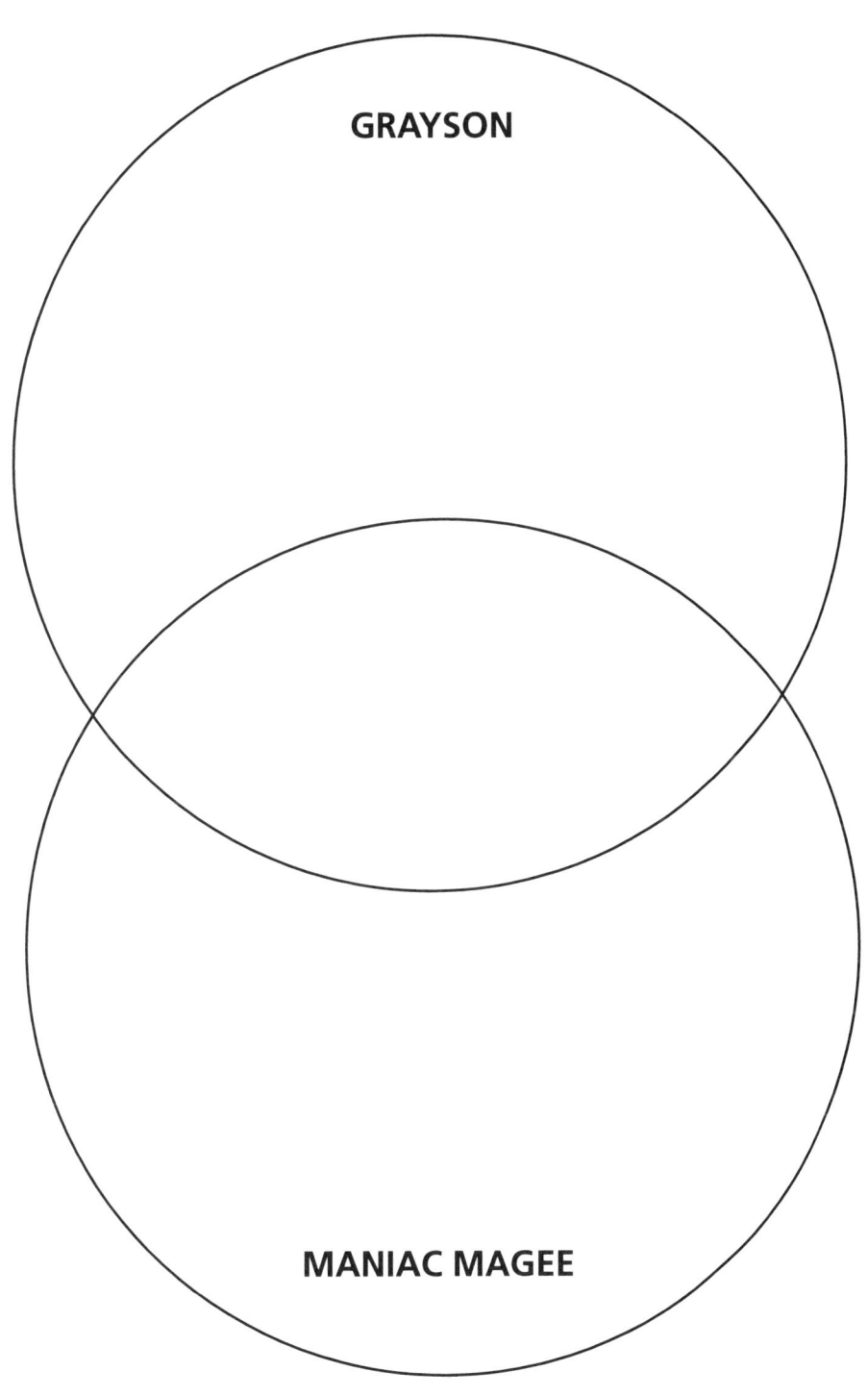

SourceBook 35

Name _____

Strategic Reading ④
SECTION 4, CHAPTERS 33–46

Analyzing Change

Characters in a work of fiction often grow or change in some way as a result of the conflicts they face. Sometimes characters change because they learn a new skill or because they are exposed to a new idea. Sometimes characters change because they develop new ways of thinking about themselves or about other people. Analyze the changes in the characters listed below, filling in the blanks in the right-hand column.

Character	What once was true	What now is true	What causes the change?
Maniac	Has a loving home with Grayson	Is hungry, homeless, and waiting to die	
John McNab	Wants to beat up Maniac	Invites Maniac home with him	
Russell and Piper	Want to run away	Agree to stay home and go to school	
Mars Bar	Seems to hate Maniac	Invites Maniac home with him	
Russell and Piper	Are afraid of African-American people	Go home with Mars Bar, play games with him, and don't want to return to their own home	
Maniac Magee	Never wants to risk being orphaned again	Agrees to go home with Amanda	

36 Literature Connections

Name _____

Literary Concept 1
CHARACTERIZATION

Characterization is the way in which writers create and develop characters' personalities. There are four basic means of character development:

- through the character's words and actions
- through the character's thoughts
- through the descriptions of the character's appearance
- through what others think of the character

To help you understand the use of characterization in *Maniac Magee,* complete the chart below as you read.

Character	Words and actions	Thoughts	Appearance	What others think
Maniac Magee				
Amanda Beale				
Mars Bar				
George McNab				
Grayson				

SourceBook 37

Name _____

Literary Concept 2
CONFLICT

A **conflict** is a struggle between opposing forces. **External conflicts** take place between a character and an outside force, such as society, a force of nature, or another character. **Internal conflicts** take place within a character's mind. The character may need to make a difficult decision or deal with conflicting feelings. In the chart below, write whether each conflict is internal or external, and then describe how the conflict is resolved.

Force	Opposing Force	Conflict
Section 1, Chapter 10 Maniac tries to protect Amanda's book.	Mars Bar says the book is his.	Type: Outcome:
Section 2, Chapter 15 Maniac talks trash inside the Beales' home.	Mrs. Beale doesn't like hearing Maniac talk that way.	Type: Outcome:
Section 3, Chapter 24 Grayson invites Maniac to live with him.	Maniac is tempted.	Type: Outcome:
Section 4, Chapter 42 Mars Bar attends Piper's birthday party.	The Cobras don't like him.	Type: Outcome:
Section 4, Chapter 46 Amanda demands that Maniac come home with her.	Maniac says he can't.	Type: Outcome:

Name _____

Literary Concept

THEME

A **theme** of a literary work is an insight or idea about life or human nature that the author shares with his or her readers. As you read *Maniac Magee,* for example, you will see that the author shares his ideas about a variety of topics, including racial prejudice, education, homelessness, and family life.

Complete the theme graphic below as you read each of the four sections of the novel. In each box, state a theme, or message, that you think the author communicates. Then list examples from the text that support your choice of theme. As a starting point, you may use one of the topics listed above, but you'll find many other options in your reading.

Section 1

Statement of theme: _____

_____

_____

Examples from the book: _____

_____

_____

_____

Section 2

Statement of theme: _____

_____

_____

Examples from the book: _____

_____

_____

_____

Section 3

Statement of theme: _____

_____

_____

Examples from the book: _____

_____

_____

_____

Section 4

Statement of theme: _____

_____

_____

Examples from the book: _____

_____

_____

_____

Name _____

Vocabulary

A. Fill in each set of blanks with the correct asterisked word from the Glossary on pages 31–32. (Clue: The boxed letters will spell the name of a character in *Maniac Magee*.)

1. Causing this can disturb others.   __ __ [__] __ __ __ __ __

2. Moving in this way might startle someone.   [__] __ __ __ __ __ __ __

3. Two or more of you do this when you come together.   __ __ [__] __ __ __ __

4. You do this when you walk with someone and then you part.   __ [__] __ __ __ __ __

5. Wearing rags and skipping baths can cause you to look like this.   __ __ __ [__] __ __ __ __

6. An object that has been handed down in your family is this.   __ __ __ __ [__] __

B. An asterisked word from the Glossary is the "I" in each of the following riddles. Write the word that answers each one.

1. Whether it's a pinecone or a carp, I describe a smell that's sharp. What am I?
   _____

2. If you have an injury to your brain, I am what you need to regain. What am I?
   _____

3. Leave others. Ignore the phone. I am what you seek when you want to be alone. What am I?
   _____

4. Of the planet Earth I am one half. If you wish to find me, don't check a graph. What am I?
   _____

5. I'm unaffected by pleasure or pain. If you try to upset me, you've nothing to gain. What am I?
   _____

6. Injuries make you move with care. Move like me when it's pain you want to spare. What am I?
   _____

7. I'm known for things that only bad. My bad reputation is ironclad. What am I?
   _____

8. I'm a good idea, a decent guess. I'm well thought of, nevertheless. What am I?
   _____

9. If you want a crowd to spread out. Mine is the name you need to shout. What am I?
   _____

10. You cannot speak. Your mind's in a haze. I describe how it feels to be amazed. What am I?
    _____

C. For each phrase at the left, write the letter of the phrase at the right that is closest in meaning.

_____ 1. walk clumsily to bed   a. rickety chickadee
_____ 2. unsteady bird   b. the urge to surge
_____ 3. the fact of long-lasting fame c. lumber to slumber
_____ 4. beg a bloodsucking worm   d. beseech a leech
_____ 5. the need to rush forward   e. the reality of immortality

40 Literature Connections

Beyond the Literature
SYNTHESIZING IDEAS

Culminating Writing Assignments

EXPLORATORY WRITING

1. Write the next **chapter** in *Maniac Magee*. Incorporate any predictions you have about what life might be like in Two Mills from now on—or about whether Maniac will be happy in his new life.
2. Write a **character sketch** of either your favorite or your least favorite character in *Maniac Magee*. Use details from the novel as well as your imagination to describe the character.
3. If the minister had arrived at Grayson's funeral on time, Maniac might have been asked to say a few words. Write the **eulogy** Maniac might have given at Grayson's funeral.
4. In the Before the Story section of the novel, the narrator says, "The history of a kid is one part fact, two parts legend, and three parts snowball." Explain what you think he means by this in an **essay,** using details and examples from the book or from your own experience to explain your point of view.

RESEARCH

1. Research the life of a major league ball player, such as Willie Mays, Babe Ruth, Jackie Robinson, or Hank Aaron. In a **research paper,** trace the player's career through the minor leagues and discuss his achievements in the majors. Try to include images of the player—copies of photographs or fine art portraits—in your paper.
2. Conduct research on the problem of illiteracy in your city or town. Try to discover how common the problem is and what's being done in your community to solve it. If possible, conduct an interview with a literacy teacher or with an adult who is learning to read and write. Summarize your findings in a **report.**

LITERARY ANALYSIS

1. Select one of the Related Readings and write an **explanation** of what it has in common with *Maniac Magee*. Think about the main themes, or messages, of the works as you look for similarities between them.
2. Read the comments of Joel Shoemaker in Critic's Corner, page 18. Write a **response essay** in which you explain why you agree or disagree with him.
3. Do you agree or disagree with the statement, "Legends are made, not born"? Defend your point of view in an **opinion paper.** Be sure to discuss whether you feel Maniac Magee was born to be a legend or whether his community turned him into one.
4. Does Maniac Magee seem like a real boy to you? What seems possible and what seems impossible about his experience? Use details from the novel as you explain your response in a short **essay.**

*For writing instruction in specific modes, have students use the **Writing Coach.**

Multimodal Activities

Jumping Rope

Invite students to return to the jump rope rhyme about Maniac on page 4 of the novel, and have them read it aloud in unison. Discuss which parts of the rhyme turn out to be true about Maniac and which parts are exaggerated. Then ask students to make up **jump rope rhymes** about some of the other characters in the novel.

Home, Sweet Home

Suggest that students create **images** of the places Maniac called "home" in the novel. They may wish to make pencil or charcoal sketches, watercolor or acrylic paintings, or collages of the places Maniac lived from the beginning to the end of the book. Have them use the novel's descriptions as well as their own imaginations to fill in the details of each place. Some students may prefer to use abstract forms to communicate Maniac's emotional state at each dwelling.

Telling the Tale

Divide the class into four groups and have each group discuss one of the novel's four sections. In preparation for an **oral retelling** of the story, ask students to think about the most important information the narrator shares and the conflicts that occur between the characters. Each group should choose a method for retelling its section of the novel. One group might present a **skit,** retelling the story through the invented dialogue of the characters; another group might share the events in a **round-robin** format.

Talk! Talk! Talk!

Stage a **radio** or **TV talk show,** with one student playing the role of Maniac Magee as the principal guest and another student playing the host. Other characters from the novel may make appearances on the show as well; the rest of the class may act as the studio audience or phone-in listeners. To prepare for the show, have students brainstorm a list of possible discussion topics based on the novel's dominant themes, such as how to get along with others, how to resolve conflicts nonviolently, or how to understand the pros and cons of different family structures.

A League of His Own

Encourage students interested in sports to work in pairs to write and then perform a **sports broadcast** on the basis of one of the athletic competitions in the novel. One student might call out the play-by-play, the other might do the "color" commentary. Have students skim *Maniac Magee* to find examples of important sports events. For example, students may wish to focus on the record-setting Little League game in which Giant John McNab strikes out 16 batters—before Maniac steps up to the plate!

Walking Tour

Small groups of students can use details about the story's setting and their own imaginations to create a **map** of Two Mills. Direct students to include such locations as characters' homes (the Beales', the McNabs', Grayson's home at the Two Mills YMCA), Hector Street, and the Schuykill River, and such points of interest as the Elmwood Park Zoo, the Little League field, Bethany Church, and Cobble's Corner Grocery. Suggest that students refer to a map of Pennsylvania that shows Norristown—Jerry Spinelli's hometown and the probable model for Two Mills.

Dream Room

Have students imagine that the Beales are adding a room to their home that will be Maniac's very own. After pairs of students review the novel to generate ideas about Maniac's personal interests and needs, have them devise a **floor plan** of Maniac's new room.

Two Mills Revisited

Assign two groups of students to present a **news report** that marks ten years since Maniac's Magee arrival in Two Mills. In each group, one student can serve as a roving reporter and others can assume the roles of various major and minor characters (for example, Hester and Lester Beale, Russell and Piper McNab). Have the reporters conduct brief interviews (using video or tape recorders, if available). Extrapolating from details in the novel, characters can share information about what has changed in the town and what has remained the same.

Cross-Curricular Projects

Who Are You?

Overview:

In this project, students will develop a stronger understanding of how family life, race, culture, and social status affect their sense of themselves. Through independent work, group discussion, and exploration through art, students will look at themselves and try to see themselves through the eyes of others. They will make connections to *Maniac Magee* as they consider how their "public face" is affected by the expectations others have of them.

Cross-Curricular Connection: Social Studies, Art

Suggested Procedure:

1. Begin the project by asking students to sketch or paint self-portraits. They may choose to sketch only their faces or to present themselves in the context of an environment, such as home or school. Display the images around the classroom and discuss the different ways in which people perceive themselves and the different messages the portraits convey.

2. Ask students to complete a web to explore who they are as individuals and the ways in which they are connected to institutions outside of themselves. For example, students' webs might be divided into sections for family members, friends, teachers and others at school, and people affiliated with a religious institution.

3. Have students share their webs in small groups and discuss ways in which students both contribute to and are supported by the stability in different areas of their lives. Connect students' thinking about identity to their reading by asking what Maniac Magee's web might look like. Draw Maniac's web on the chalkboard if students offer ideas. Have students note the differences between the webs.

4. Ask students to think about the ways in which other people describe or label them. Ask them to think about whether they live up to those labels and to think generally about how labels affect the way people behave. For example, if a person is described by others as a bully, does the person choose to disobey the rules and live up to that label as an aggressor? Allow students time to freewrite in their notebooks about this issue. They may wish to focus on the way in which Mars Bar Thompson lived up to the many rumors about him.

5. Have students sketch or paint a second self-portrait, trying to present themselves as others see them. Display these portraits beside the original portraits students created, and discuss the differences between them. Hold a discussion about public and private perceptions. Make connections to their reading by sharing ideas about who characters are and who others perceive them to be (for example, Grayson).

Teaching Tip

Offer students the option of presenting their self-portraits to classmates or reserving them in portfolios for your review.

Living on the Streets: No Life at All

Overview:

In this project, students will consider the problem of homelessness from different angles. They will learn about homeless populations in other countries and cultures and study homelessness during the Depression in this country. Students will compare what they learn with the information presented in *Maniac Magee*. Students will study available resources and conduct a fundraising campaign for a local homeless shelter.

Cross-Curricular Connection: Social Studies, Art, Math

Suggested Procedure:

1. Have students do some focused freewriting in their notebooks about how they might feel if they found themselves without a home to return to after school. Ask students to write about what would bother them most about being homeless.

2. Divide students into small groups and have them conduct research on the problem of homelessness in other parts of the world, such as India, South America, or Central America. Have at least one group research the history of homelessness in the United States, focusing perhaps on the Great Depression. Groups should present their findings to the class in oral reports. Discuss the fact that homelessness is not a new problem, nor is it confined to individual neighborhoods, cities, or countries.

3. Have students do research on the homeless in their communities. Have them try to uncover who is homeless, why, and what their lives are like. Ask students to consider why it's so difficult to accurately count how many homeless people there are.

4. Have students create a public service announcement (or PSA) for television or radio that encourages people to resist the tendency to become insensitive to the plight of the homeless. If your school broadcasts through cable or other local stations, have students tailor their PSA to that audience. Ask students to consider how an important issue like homelessness, which requires ongoing support, can become overshadowed when another issue gets the attention of the public.

5. Have students organize a fundraising campaign for the homeless in their community. Students can use the money they raise to support the efforts of a local homeless shelter or a related service organization. Have students work in small groups to brainstorm ways to raise money. Students can focus on a single event or plan a series of them over a period of time. Then have students form teams to do the necessary research and to make posters and flyers. At a fundraising event, students can take turns managing a general information table, sharing what they know about the area's homeless population. The shelter or service that students choose to support might co-sponsor an event by supplying their own information and mailing materials.

Teaching Tip

During students' brainstorming session, you might offer some of these suggestions:

- sell crafts
- create and sell a theme-based calendar
- organize a car wash
- write fundraising letters
- conduct a food or clothing drive.

Suggestions for Assessment

Negotiated Rubrics

Negotiating rubrics for assessment with students allows them to know before they start an assignment what is required and how it will be judged, and gives them additional ownership of the final product. A popular method of negotiating rubrics is for the teacher and students individually to list the qualities that the final product should contain, then compare the teacher-generated list with the student-generated list and together decide on a compromise.

Portfolio Building

Remind students that they have many choices of types of assignments to select for their portfolios. Among these are the following:

- Culminating Writing Assignments (page 41)
- Writing Prompts, found in the Discussion Starters
- Multimodal Activities (pages 42–43)
- Cross-Curricular Projects (pages 44–45)

Suggest that students use some of the following questions as criteria in selecting which pieces to include in their portfolios.

- Which shows my clearest thinking about the literature?
- Which is or could become most complete?
- Which shows a type of work not presently included in my portfolio?
- Which am I proudest of?

Remind students to reflect on the pieces they choose and to attach a note explaining why they included each and how they would evaluate it.

For suggestions on how to assess portfolios, see **Teacher's Guide to Assessment and Portfolio Use.**

Writing Assessment

The following can be made into formal assignments for evaluation:

- Culminating Writing Assignments page 41
- A written analysis of the Critic's Corner literary criticism
- Fully developed Writing Prompts from the Discussion Starters

For rubrics to help you evaluate specific kinds of writing, see **The Guide to Writing Assessment** *in the* **Formal Assessment** *booklet of* **The Language of Literature.**

Test

The test on pages 47–48 consists of essay and short-answer questions. The answer key follows.

Alternative Assessment

For the kinds of authentic assessments found on many state and districtwide tests, see the **Alternative Assessment** booklet of *The Language of Literature.*

46 Literature Connections

Name

Date

Test

Maniac Magee **and Related Readings**

Essay

Choose two of the following essay questions to answer on your own paper. (25 points each)

1. Do you think it is a good idea for Maniac to invite Mars Bar to spend time with him in the town's West End? Use examples from the novel to explain why or why not. Consider the kind of person Mars Bar reveals himself to be in the beginning of the book, what he learns from his experiences in the West End, and what happens at the novel's end.

2. At the book's end, Maniac "knew that finally, truly, at long last, someone was calling him home." What does "home" mean to Maniac? Does he have a home with Grayson? Use examples from the novel to answer these questions and to show how he knows that he has truly found a home with Amanda Beale and her family.

3. Explain Maniac's opinions about school and learning. Why does Maniac insist that Russell and Piper go to school, even though he doesn't go to school himself? Predict whether Maniac will ever go to school again, and explain why or why not.

4. Compare and contrast Two Mills with the city or town in which you live. Before you begin writing, you may wish to explore your ideas using a Venn diagram like the one shown below. List the things the two communities have in common in the space where the two circles intersect.

5. Compare *Maniac Magee* to one of the Related Readings in this Literature Connections anthology. You may wish to compare the two works by focusing on a specific literary element, such as characterization, conflict, or theme.

SourceBook 47

Name _____

Date _____

Test (continued)

Maniac Magee and Related Readings

Short Answer

On your paper, write a short answer for each question below and give a reason for your answer. (5 points each)

1. Why or why don't you think that Jeffrey Lionel Magee does the right thing by running away from his aunt and uncle's home?

2. Why does Jeffrey prefer to be called by his given name instead of by his nickname, Maniac?

3. Describe the affect Maniac has on Mrs. Beale, Amanda, and the twins, Hester and Lester, when he lives with them in Section 2.

4. The man yelling at Maniac at the block party in Section 2 says, "The sheep lie not with the lion! The sheep knows his own! His own kind!" What does he mean?

5. What does Amanda think will happen if Maniac unties Cobble's Knot?

6. Grayson gives Maniac small amounts of money each day. Why does he spend it the way he does?

7. Why do Grayson and Maniac enjoy spending time with one another?

8. Why does Maniac walk away from the trestle instead of rescuing Russell?

9. Why do you think Russell clings to Mars Bar and then to Mars Bar's mother after he is rescued?

10. How can you explain Maniac Magee's relationship with the animals at the zoo?

Test Answer Key

Maniac Magee and Related Readings

Essay

Answers to essay questions will vary, but opinions should be stated clearly and supported by details from the text. Suggestions for points to look for are given below.

1. Students who think that it isn't a good idea to bring Mars Bar into the West End may say:

   - Mars could have been hurt by angry Cobras.

   - It's unfair of Maniac to think Mars will be accepted by everyone in that part of town.

   - Given the hostility Mars feels toward Maniac throughout most of the book, he probably feels that way about other whites as well.

   - Even though Mars and Maniac get along in the end, Mars's visit to the West End does little toward bridging the town's racial divide.

   Students who think that it is a good idea to bring Mars Bar into the West End may say:

   - It's important for Mars to learn the same lesson about race that Maniac learns: that there are some people who will treat everyone with dignity and respect (the Pickwells, the Beales) and there are some who will treat others with hatred and disrespect (the McNabs, the angry man at the block party)

   - Mars learns that Maniac is on his side after Maniac protects him at the McNabs

   - The visit goes a long way toward bridging the town's racial divide: in the end, the Pickwell children and Mars get to know one another, Mars and Maniac become friends, and Russell and Piper spend time with a loving African-American family. None of this would have been possible unless Maniac had taken a risk.

2. For Maniac, home is a place where people talk to each other, sharing meals and games and love. It is also a place for both parents (who behave like responsible adults) and children. Some may say that Maniac does have a home with Grayson because he has shelter and Grayson takes good care of him, providing him with food and clothing and spending money. He certainly has more of a home there than the McNab kids ever have with their father. Others may say that you can't call the equipment room at a bandshell home, that Maniac doesn't receive any discipline, and that he doesn't get to live like a normal kid. At the Beales' house, Maniac will get what he wants and needs: siblings and parents who will love him, care for him, talk to him, discipline him, play with him, teach him.

3. Maniac is an avid learner, spending all his spare change on books at the library. The world is his school. Maniac learns more about life—getting to know social norms in Two Mills and sharing a room with Grayson—than he would if he had been in a classroom. Maniac does, however, see the importance of school and schooling. He insists Russell and Piper go to school for a variety of reasons. He knows that school is the only place the two will receive care and discipline; he sees that the children will only get into trouble or run away if they play hooky. Maniac sees an important connection between home and school, however. He feels you can't have one without the other; it's likely that after he gets settled at the Beales' house, he will return to school.

Test Answer Key (continued)

Maniac Magee and Related Readings

4. Answers will vary. Students are likely to compare the relative racial integration or segregation of their towns or communities; the ways people treat others; the prevalence of homelessness and illiteracy; the importance of sports and competition in their lives, and so on.

5. Students should focus on characterization, conflict, or theme as they compare the novel with one of the related readings. Students may touch on the following ideas as they consider the readings:

   - from *Freedom's Children:* what it's like and how it feels to live in a world divided by race

   - "Where the Rainbow Ends": visions for a better world where race doesn't matter and people live in harmony

   - "Those Who Don't": learning what it's like to be on the outside looking in; how it feels to be a minority

   - "A Lesson for Kings": new ways of defining power and courage

   - "The Boy with Yellow Eyes": Norman's love of books and learning; what happens when people make assumptions about other people and believe rumors about them

   - "Runner": running theme and connection with the natural world

   - "Final Curve": understanding, self-awareness

   - "Stormalong": restlessness; wandering; difficulty fitting in with others; legendary status

Short Answer

Answers will vary but should reflect the following ideas.

1. Jeffrey runs away because his aunt and uncle hate each other and haven't said a word to each other since Jeffrey came to live with them. Jeffrey runs because for him, a loveless home like this is worse than no home at all. Some students will say that Jeffrey did the right thing because in the end, he found a loving home; others will say that he should have stayed and talked more directly with his aunt and uncle about the problems he was having.

2. Jeffrey prefers to be called by his given name because it is truly all he has left from his parents; it's the only evidence he has that he was once loved and cared for. He acquires the name Maniac because of the things he does, not because of who he is. And humble Jeffrey doesn't seem to think that his actions are all that special anyway.

3. Thanks to Maniac, Mrs. Beale no longer spends her days with a sponge in her hand, wiping up after Hester and Lester. In fact, Maniac gives her a hand with many household chores, which makes her life much easier. Maniac helps Amanda—though she'd hate to admit it—by sleeping in her room. This allows her to snuggle in bed with her little brother and sister. And Hester and Lester benefit from having someone to take baths with them and read to them.

50 Literature Connections

Test Answer Key (continued)

Maniac Magee and Related Readings

4. Paraphrasing from scripture, the man is telling Maniac that people of different races—black and white—should not mix. Like animals in the animal kingdom who "know their own kind," white-skinned people like Maniac should stay on the West End with other whites.

5. Amanda thinks that if Maniac unties Cobble's Knot, he will become a local hero, loved and admired by people on both ends of town. His picture will appear in the paper, he'll be famous in Two Mills, and no one will "mess" with him again.

6. Maniac goes to the public library and buys used books with the money Grayson gives him. Maniac loves books and learning, and he buys many different types of books—from math books to cookbooks—to further his education.

7. Maniac and Grayson seem to enjoy every minute they spend together. They have much in common and they each bring new things to the relationship. The two share a love and respect for the game of baseball. They had similarly difficult childhoods, and they are both grateful for the friendship and companionship of another person after spending so many years alone. Maniac teaches Grayson to read; Grayson teaches Maniac about baseball. They teach each other about love.

8. In all the time he's spent running in and around Two Mills and Bridgeport, Maniac has not been able to bring himself even to look at the trestle, the site where his parents were killed in a trolley accident. Maniac has not yet come to terms with his parents' loss, and looking out on the trestle means reliving the painful nightmare of their deaths.

9. At first Russell clings to Mars Bar out of both fear and gratitude for having been saved. The fact that he clings to Mars Bar's mother shows how starved he is for a mother's love and affection.

10. Maniac is an extremely compassionate boy. He's very observant and considerate of others—including animals—treating them the way he'd want to be treated. Maniac may be envious of the animals because they have what he lacks: a permanent home in which they are well fed and cared for.

Additional Resources

Other Works by Jerry Spinelli

Space Station Seventh Grade. 1982.
Seventh grader Jason Herkimer discovers that junior high has its good and bad points when he scuffles with a female trombone player, endures gym-class showers, makes moose calls in assembly, and falls in love.

Who Put That Hair in My Toothbrush? 1984.
Twelve-year-old Meg and her teenage brother, Greg, cannot seem to get along. They share their stories in alternating first person narratives.

Night of the Whale. 1985.
A group of six rowdy high school seniors staying at a beach house grow up quickly when they discover an extraordinary number of beached whales.

Jason and Marceline. 1986.
In the sequel to *Space Station Seventh Grade,* Jason tries to cope with three important things in his life: his relationship with Marceline McAllister, his peer group, and his burgeoning sexuality.

Dump Days. 1988.
On the first morning of the first day of their summer vacation, two friends decide to have an absolutely perfect day before the summer ends.

The Bathwater Gang. 1990.
Bertie's all-girl gang becomes involved in a harmless but heartfelt war with an all-boy gang, until Bertie's grandmother steps in with a perfect solution.

Report to the Principal's Office. 1991.
Four totally different kids have only one thing in common—they're all about to report to the principal's office.

There's a Girl in My Hammerlock. 1991.
Thirteen-year-old Maisie joins her school's formerly all-male wrestling team and tries to last through the season, despite opposition from other students, her best friend, and her own teammates.

Fourth Grade Rats. 1991.
Suds learns that his best friend is wrong. You don't have to be a tough guy, a "rat," to be a grown up fourth grader.

The Bathwater Gang Gets Down to Business. 1992.
When the Bathwater Gang fails to make money with its pet-cleaning business, Bertie comes up with a slightly dishonest idea to ensure success.

Tooter Pepperday. 1995.
Hating to leave her familiar surroundings, Tooter resorts to sabotage when her family moves from their suburban home to Aunt Sally's farm.

Crash. 1996.
John "Crash" Coogan enjoys living up to his nickname. A family crisis and an experience with an unusual Quaker boy cause Crash to take a hard look at his aggressive nature.

FICTION

Carlson, Natalie Savage. *The Family Under the Bridge.* New York: Harper, 1989. This award-winning novel about the friendship between an old hobo and a homeless family in Paris was originally published in 1958. **(challenging)**

Colman, Hila. *Claudia, Where Are You?* New York: Morrow, 1969. 16-year-old Claudia runs away from her parents' suburban home to live in New York City. In alternating chapters, the author presents both the parents' anguish and the excitement and perils of Claudia's new life. **(average)**

Crutcher, Chris. *The Crazy Horse Electric Game.* New York: Greenwillow Books, 1987. High school baseball star Willie Weaver can no longer compete after he is injured in a water-skiing accident. He runs away and ends up at a tough alternative school, where he regains his lost self-esteem. **(average)**

Gallo, Donald, R., ed. *Ultimate Sports: Short Stories by Outstanding Writers for Young Adults.* New York: Delacorte, 1995. Such notables as Robert Lipsyte and Chris Lynch contribute original stories covering a wide range of sports. **(easy)**

Micklish, Rita. *Sugar Bee.* New York: Delacorte, 1972. A young African-American city girl visits a white family in the country in this novel about interracial friendship. **(average)**

Tunis, John R. *The Kid from Tomkinsville.* New York: Scholastic, 1992. This classic story of a young pitcher for the Brooklyn Dodgers was originally published in 1940. Roy Tucker helps pull his team out of a slump before a freak accident ends his career as a pitcher; Roy must find another place for himself on the team. **(average)**

NONFICTION

Higginsen, Vy. *This Is My Song!: A Collection of Gospel Music for the Family.* New York: Crown, 1995. This introduction to gospel music includes authentic arrangements of 32 songs. **(average)**

Myers, Walter Dean. *Now Is Your Time!: The African-American Struggle for Freedom.* New York: HarperCollins, 1991. A history of the African-American struggle for freedom and equality beginning with the capture of Africans in 1619, continuing through the American Revolution and the Civil War, and ending in contemporary times. Combines historical survey, biography, storytelling, and family history. **(challenging)**

MULTIMEDIA

And the Children Shall Lead. Video Recording. Wonderworks, 1985. Distributed by Public Media Video. Color. 60 min. Starring Danny Glover and LeVar Burton. A young girl joins the struggle for equality when civil-rights activists arrive in her small Mississippi town. **(videocassette)**

A Class Divided. Video Recording. PBS Video, 1985. Color. 60 min. A combination of film from the original FRONTLINE documentary and a reunion of former third-graders who participated in a powerful experiment in which the all-white class was divided into blue-and brown-eyed groups for a lesson in discrimination. **(videocassette)**

Eyes on the Prize—The Commemorative Edition. 1987–1990. B&W/Color. 840 min. 14 cassettes. This edition includes all 14 one-hour episodes of the documentary on the American civil rights movement. It also includes a hard-cover companion book by Henry Hampton and a compact disc of civil rights songs of the era. (*videocassette, book, CD*)

The History of Baseball. Video Recording. Major League Baseball Properties, Inc., 1987. Under license by the Phoenix Communications Group, Inc. Contains the complete history of baseball, from its beginnings as a game for children to the 26 major league teams of today. 120 min. **(videocassette)**

Kids and Race: Working it Out. Video Recording. Films for the Humanities. Color. 52 min. Presents nine young people taking part in a weekend encounter group to talk about the feelings that stereotypes and prejudice create. **(videocassette)**

Maniac Magee. Video Recording. Chatsworth, CA: AIMS Media, 1992. Color. 30 min. **(videocassette)**

Pride and Prejudice: A History of Black Culture in America. 1994. Noted author Clifton Taulbert follows the turbulent history of blacks in America as they struggled for civil rights. **(videocassette)**

Runaway. Video Recording. Wonderworks, 1989. Distributed by Public Media Video. Color. 58 min. After a gang kills his only friend, a boy seeks refuge in the subway system of New York. A Vietnam veteran and a coffee shop waitress help him to survive in the treacherous world of the homeless. Adapted from the novel Slake's Limbo by Felice Holman. **(videocassette)**

Sports Pages: 1950s Baseball Dream Team. Video Recording. Combined Artists, 1991. Distributed by Simitar Entertainment, Inc., Plymouth, MN. 30 min. Baseball stars Willie Mays, Mickey Mantle, Hank Aaron, Jackie Robinson, Yogi Bera, and more are profiled in this program. **(videocassette)**

Storytellers: Tall Tales, Yarns, and Whoppers. 35 min. Giant animals, superhuman feats, and other preposterous impossibilities make these stories very entertaining for all ages. **(videocassette)**

Struggles for Justice: Vol. 1. Emerging Technology Consultants, Inc. Helps viewers relive the trials and triumphs faced by Native, Hispanic, and African Americans in the United States. **(videodisc)**

Trolley—The Cars That Built Our Cities. 1991. A complete history of the American trolley in photographs, from the 1890s to the 1990s. Color. 60 min. **(videocassette)**